TELL ME WHY

The Moon Is More Than a Night-Light

illustrated by

ROBERT E. WELLS

PATRICK CORRIGAN

Albert Whitman & Company
Chicago, Illinois

For Pia, Jules, Henry, and Honoré—REW

For Matthew—PC

Library of Congress Cataloging-in-Publication data is on file with the publisher.
Text copyright © 2022 by Robert E. Wells
Illustrations copyright © 2022 by Albert Whitman & Company
Illustrations by Patrick Corrigan
First published in the United States of America in 2022 by Albert Whitman & Company
ISBN 978-0-8075-5275-9 (hardcover) • ISBN 978-0-8075-5276-6 (ebook)
Printed in China
10 9 8 7 6 5 4 3 2 1 WKT 26 25 24 23 22
Design by Aphelandra
For more information about Albert Whitman & Company, please visit our website at www.albertwhitman.com.

The moon is Earth's natural night-light. Its bright glow can help an owl spot its prey and make your walk safer on a dark path through the woods.

But the moon is more than just a night-light. The pull of its gravity does many important things that help us live on planet Earth.

Gravity is a natural force in the universe.
Earth's gravity pulls people, dogs, and anything else
with weight down toward the center of the planet.

Earth's gravity also pulls on the moon,
keeping it orbiting, or traveling around, Earth.
The moon's gravity pulls the earth toward
the moon at the same time, but because
Earth is bigger, it pulls harder.

Earth

moon

Meanwhile, both Earth and our moon orbit the sun. Earth also rotates, or spins, around an imaginary line through its middle, called an axis.

sun

moon's orbit
around Earth

Earth's orbit
around sun

The pull of the moon's gravity helps to steady Earth's rotation. Without that stability, scientists believe that Earth's weather might have been too wild and stormy for most living things to survive.

Earth's axis

N

S

The moon's gravity keeps Earth's axis tilted at a just-right angle of 23.5 degrees.

This angle causes the sun to shine on different parts of Earth as it orbits, making days, nights, and seasons happen at different times in different places around the planet.

The moon's gravity also pulls on Earth's oceans, causing tides. Tides move ocean water back and forth on beaches, allowing sand to clean the water by absorbing toxic poisons and pollution.

The motion of tides also mixes air, water, and food into oceans, helping sea creatures grow. These creatures become food for people and animals.

By creating tides and stabilizing Earth, the moon's gravity supports all living things. The moon's changing appearance also helped early people measure time.

Before modern clocks and calendars were invented, ancient Egyptian farmers learned when to plant and harvest crops by keeping track of the moon's shapes, or phases.

In those days, people did not know that the moon only appeared to change shape. In reality, the sun simply shines on the moon in different places as the moon orbits Earth.

The Egyptians observed that about twenty-nine and a half days passed between each appearance of a full moon. Our word *month* comes from the word *moon*.

When the first telescope was built in 1608, people began to learn more about the moon because they could see it better. Astronomers spent many hours observing the moon with telescopes, drawing pictures and writing about what they saw.

But even with the aid of telescopes, most of the moon's mysteries were still unsolved. After all, no one had ever been there!

The moon is Earth's closest neighbor in space, but it still orbits at a distance of about 240,000 miles. Can you imagine a journey that far? It would be like traveling around Earth almost ten times!

In the late 1950s and early 1960s, traveling to the moon began to seem possible. To get there, a rocket would first have to escape the strong pull of Earth's gravity and then fly close enough to the moon for the moon's gravity to pull it the rest of the way.

The United States' Saturn V rocket was designed and built for that journey. It is still the tallest and most powerful rocket ever to operate. It stood about thirty-six stories high!

USA

In July 1969, the Apollo 11 mission carried the first space travelers to land on another world—our moon. Astronauts began to collect moon rocks for scientists to study back on Earth and learn more about the moon's history. Over the next three years, five more Apollo missions landed on the moon, gathering more than 800 pounds of moon rocks for scientists to study.

In the 1990s and 2000s, uncrewed moon missions equipped with scientific instruments sent back surprising new information to Earth's scientists: there is frozen water on the moon!

Finding water on the moon was an important discovery. Water is essential for space travelers to drink and can also be divided into its chemical elements—hydrogen and oxygen.

People breathe oxygen and could use hydrogen as rocket fuel, so water could allow the moon to be used as a base for future space travelers exploring other parts of the solar system.

With the information discovered in moon rocks brought back to Earth, scientists have learned more about how the moon was formed.

Most scientists now believe that about 4.5 billion years ago, as Earth was forming, a planet-sized asteroid collided with it.

The collision blasted trillions of tons of rocks and dust into orbit. The rocks and dust joined together into bigger clumps, which eventually formed our moon.

More clumps joined Earth and gave it a large metal core. The swirling molten metal inside Earth generates a magnetic shield around our planet, protecting life from harmful cosmic rays in space.

Ever since the moon was created, it has been a valuable companion and helper to life on Earth.

The collision between early Earth and the giant asteroid also made Earth's crust, or outer layer, thinner. Compared to its overall size, Earth's crust is about as thin as the skin on an apple.

Because this crust is thin, it began to crack, dividing Earth's surface into what scientists call tectonic plates. As these plates moved slowly against each other, they caused land to rise above oceans.

tectonic plates

If not for its tectonic plates, Earth's surface would still be completely covered with ocean water. Our planet would be a good home for sea creatures—but not for people.

ocean water

Just imagine! If our moon had not been created by that asteroid impact so long ago, Earth would be a very different planet. The creation of our moon, and the pull of its gravity, have made life as we know it possible.

On top of all that, the moon
is a really nice night-light!

Glossary

astronomer: a scientist who studies planets, stars, and other objects outside of Earth's atmosphere

axis: an imaginary line through the center of an object, around which the object revolves like a spinning top

orbit: to travel in a curved path around an object, like the path of the moon as it travels around Earth

tectonic plates: the large areas of Earth's crust, or outer layer, which are divided into sections and move gradually over Earth's inner layers

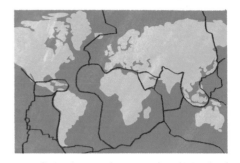

telescope: a tool, usually shaped like a tube, designed to make distant objects appear bigger

tides: the movement of water caused by the gravitational pulls of the moon and sun

Selected Sources

Gribbin, John. *Alone in the Universe*. Hoboken, NJ: John Wiley and Sons, 2011.

Leatherbarrow, Bill. *The Moon*. London: Reaktion Books, 2018.

Scott, Elaine. *Our Moon*. New York: Clarion Books, 2015.

"Special Report: 50th Anniversary of Apollo 11." *Scientific American*, July 2019: 50–83.

"The New Moon." *Discover*, May 2010: 59–64.

"To the Moon and Back." *Discover*, June 2019: 34–53.